A WALK ON KASHMIR

Heaven on Earth

Akshat Thapa

Notion Press

Old No. 38, New No. 6
McNichols Road, Chetpet
Chennai - 600 031

First Published by Notion Press 2019
Copyright © Akshat Thapa 2019
All Rights Reserved.

ISBN 978-1-64587-221-4

One day I have decided to spend time on Kashmir so I packed my bag and begins my journey towards Kashmir and find some facts & files of Heaven on Earth.

A Morning begins in God gifted valley known as heaven on earth (Kashmir). The place which is been full with nature the place known for his beauty. A best place which is been make with passions by god each and every place shows the beauty and relaxing zone on earth. The place where no medicine required the fresh air and the beauty itself is the medicine for any cure.

But on the second thought there is one more Kashmir which people are not knowing who didn't live here only listen the various talks on Kashmir various debates are been there for Kashmir but there is no solution yet been made for "Heaven on Earth."

Its a bitter truth that In free India still Kashmir is not free. Yes it really very sad to hear but its true. In this book of mine I will take you to the journey of "Heaven on Earth." I will take you towards various good and bad aspect of Kashmir in my various chapter.

Contents

History on Kashmir

When you want to write on any topic is must to begins with history. So in my first chapter I begins with the history with the history only I will try to find with facts and figures of Kashmir. And make you aware with this in detail how the Kashmir is been formed and what are the issue is been came over.

Islamabad and New Delhi are certainly saying nothing new as far as their respective stances on Kashmir are concerned. Yet it is quite clear that the conflict in and about this long-disputed region is back on centre stage—and not entirely because of Pakistan's efforts. Kashmiris have launched a non-violent agitation movement since 2010 amid arrests, custodial deaths and relentless military oppression. They have, indeed, paid a very heavy price for many decades to get their story across to the world.

For the most part, Kashmir has been known to people through state representations. This is true for Kashmir's history and perhaps equally so for the policies of the two states towards it. Both Islamabad and New Delhi ceaselessly try to expunge from public imagination anything that questions, albeit remotely, their official narratives on Kashmir even when the two narratives sometimes are as divergent from truth as they are from each other. Some of their most glaring contradictions and lies came to the surface for the first time when India's Ministry of External Affairs recently declassified its archived documents, covering 50 years of the country's foreign relations starting with 1947.

Kashmir's story, as presented here on, is mainly reconstructed through those declassified documents. Where the documents are not available, especially for the post-1997 era, the narrative is continued by citing other primary sources. What follows is a historical account of the tragedy of Kashmir. A tragedy that stems from a ceaseless contestation for a pursuit based on two arbitrary – and conflicting – claims put forth by Pakistan and India.

Some details talk on Delhi 1947: It was supposed to be a new world that Lord Mountbatten traversed in those last months of 1947 as British India's last viceroy. The Indian subcontinent, so long the jewel in Great Britain's imperial crown, had been born anew and transformed into two sovereign states. And yet, as he made his way from Delhi to Karachi, it must have occurred to Mountbatten how little things had actually changed. Decades of nationalist struggle, two world wars, a formal transfer of power and millions of deaths later, he still had to mediate between the leaders of the new subcontinent. They were still grappling with – and fighting over – a number of unanswered questions. Perched on the very top of those questions was the one of Kashmir.

The British Raj in the Indian subcontinent had always been a highly complicated affair. To run an imperial enterprise spread over half a continent, the

British authorities had to create and maintain several types of territorial arrangements, much like the Mughals before it. The British had to weave an intricate web of local collaborations that included a buffer zone between India and Afghanistan, hundreds of princely states of various sizes, that had a certain degree of legal and administrative autonomy from the Raj within their borders, and many directly administered provinces and territories. The decolonisation process spelled the unravelling of this web. The two new states – India and Pakistan – that emerged from the decolonisation process could not operate under the same legal, political and administrative paradigm which the British had. The geographical unity of the two states could only be maintained if they came up with new political and legal arrangements to integrate swathes of territory, both big and small, that once belonged to the princely states. In order to deal with this challenge, the two states embarked on projects to absorb such territories into their respective borders as quickly as possible. There was no universally acknowledged single instrument to achieve this. Both states used a similar repertoire of techniques—negotiating accession treaties, making deals with local elites and, in certain cases, sending in troops to snuff out opposition.

The Kashmir crisis was born out of the discontents of the twin processes of decolonisation and territorial integration by India and Pakistan. Jammu and Kashmir was a princely state which the East India Company had annexed in 1846 and then transferred to Gulab Singh of the Dogra dynasty for a payment of 7,500,000 rupees. As the British exit from the subcontinent became apparent, the then ruler of Jammu and Kashmir,

Hari Singh, wished to remain independent. This was obviously not going to be acceptable to either India or Pakistan. Four major rivers originate from the Himalayas located in Kashmir and it also shares a border with China—the two factors that make it a strategically crucial region. In other words it is a prized territory. Both states, therefore, formed strategies to lay claim to it.

India's deputy prime minister Sardar Vallabhbhai Patel received an urgent letter from Prime Minister Jawaharlal Nehru regarding the situation in Kashmir. Nehru was convinced that Pakistan was preparing to infiltrate the region and foster an insurgency. He also knew Maharaja Hari Singh's forces could not do much to stop infiltration without help from India. More importantly, Nehru realised, Hari Singh's regime could not be sustained if its own people went against it.

Sheikh Abdullah headed the largest political party in Kashmir – the National Conference – but he was a staunch opponent of the Dogra dynasty. He had initiated a "Quit Kashmir" movement before the British left India in 1947 and, hence, was imprisoned in May 1946. Nehru wanted him freed. He noted in his letter that Sheikh Abdullah was eager not to join Pakistan. His opposition to Hari Singh, therefore, was not tantamount to support for accession to Pakistan. If the Indian government could work out a rapprochement between Hari Singh and Sheikh Abdullah, Nehru suggested to Patel, Kashmir's accession to India would become easier. "It seems to me urgently necessary, therefore, that the accession to the Indian Union should take place early. It is equally clear to me that this can only take place with some measure of success after there is peace between the Maharaja and the National Conference and they co-operate together to meet the situation," Nehru wrote. "… Abdullah is very anxious to keep out of Pakistan and relies upon us a great deal for advice." But, at the same time, he "cannot carry his people with him unless he has something definite to place before them. What this can be in the circumstances I cannot define precisely at the present moment. But the main thing is that the Maharaja should try to gain the goodwill and cooperation of Abdullah," Nehru added. "It would be a tragedy if the National Conference remains passive owing to frustration and lack of opportunity."

Nehru's predictions about a likely infiltration into Kashmir were proven true. By October 1947, tribal militias from Murree, Hazara and parts of the Federally Administered Tribal Areas (Fata) raided the valley through the Poonch area and began a widespread campaign to destabilise the Maharaja's regime. The Maharaja looked to India for help which he got only after promising to sign an instrument of accession in favour of New Delhi.

Writing to British Prime Minister Clement Attlee, Nehru argued that the Indian intervention in Kashmir was a response to an urgent appeal from the government of Jammu and Kashmir for help against tribal invaders who, he claimed, were aided and abetted by the Pakistani government.

Pakistan denied any involvement. Prime Minister Liaquat Ali Khan insisted the actions by the tribesmen were an almost instinctive response to the atrocities being committed against Muslims in Kashmir. In his correspondence with Nehru, he argued that the tribesmen were helped by local Kashmiri Muslims who sought liberation. Liaquat Ali Khan also pointed out that the government in Kashmir had manipulated the situation in order to accede to India against the wishes of its own people. For Governor General Muhammad Ali Jinnah, the accession was nothing short of a coup d'etat.

A different story hid behind these public statements. On November 1, 1947, Mountbatten and his chief of staff, Lord Ismay, travelled to Lahore and met separately with both Jinnah and Liaquat Ali Khan. When he recorded the daily proceedings in his notebook, Mountbatten could not help but say the tribesmen had been acting on the express and direct command of the Pakistani leadership. Implicitly, Jinnah accepted as much to Mountbatten. "When I asked him how the tribesmen were to be called off, he said that all he had to do was to give them an order to come out and to warn them that if they did not comply, he would send large forces along their lines of communication. In fact, if I was prepared to fly to Srinagar with him, he would guarantee that the business would be settled within 24 hours. I expressed mild astonishment at the degree of control that he appeared to exercise over the raiders," Mountbatten wrote.

Pakistani strategy was to create enough pressure on the Maharaja to abdicate, to then claim that the region should become a part of Pakistan because most people living in Jammu and Kashmir are Muslims. The Pakistani government knew only an indigenous revolt could preclude India from holding on to Kashmir. But therein lay Pakistan's greatest challenge: The Muslim League had virtually no presence in the state of Jammu and Kashmir and Pakistan had no guarantee that the people of Kashmir would overwhelmingly vote to be part of Pakistan.

Pakistani leadership was aware of the problem which is why both Jinnah and Liaquat Ali Khan consistently rejected a plebiscite in Kashmir as long as Indian troops were there. "If the India Government [is] allowed to act...unfettered as [it pleases] by virtue of having already occupied Kashmir and landed their troops there, then, this *El Dorado* of plebiscite will prove a mirage," read an official Pakistan statement. During negotiations with Mountbatten, Jinnah strongly objected to having a plebiscite even under the auspices of the UN, maintaining that the presence of Indian troops as well as Sheikh Abdullah's tilt towards India would deter the average Muslim in Kashmir from voting for Pakistan. In a letter to Attlee, Liaquat Ali Khan described Sheikh Abdullah as a "quisling" and a "paid agent of the Congress for the last two decades."

In a December 1947 meeting with his Indian counterpart, Liaquat Ali Khan also questioned the efficacy of a voting process in Kashmir while it was under an India-sponsored administration. "...[T]he people of Kashmir were bound to vote, in the plebiscite, in favour of whatever administration was then in power. The Kashmiris were an illiterate and oppressed people, and they would be bound to favor the authority in possession. If an Englishman went as administrator, they would vote to join the United Kingdom," he said.

That not only the Maharaja but also the National Conference favoured India was the advantage Nehru wanted. In his correspondence with Indian politicians, he pointed out that any activity by Pakistan would look illegal and unacceptable after Kashmir had acceded to India. He was right. After the Maharaja acceded to India on October 26, 1947, New Delhi was successful in portraying to the rest of the world that Pakistan-supported militant activity was an act of belligerence. This would remain the thrust of India's case against Pakistan for the times to come.

The accession also formed the basis for a justification of India's military presence in Kashmir. The Indian government argued it was well within its right to send troops to drive away outsiders from what it considered Indian territory. When Pakistan contended that it would only attempt to ensure the withdrawal of tribal militias if that coincided with a simultaneous withdrawal of Indian forces from Kashmir, the Indians simply refused, arguing that the presence of the two forces could not be treated the same way.

By the end of 1947, India decided to apprise the world of what it called Pakistani intrusion in Kashmir. In a meeting with Mountbatten in December that year, Nehru suggested India should raise the issue at the United Nations Security Council (UNSC), "charging Pakistan with aggression and asking UNO [United Nations Organization] to call upon Pakistan to refrain from doing so." If the Security Council failed to make Pakistan stop its "aggression," he warned, "we would have to take action ourselves in such a manner as we thought fit to stop this aggression at the base."

When Mountbatten suggested that the "UNO [should] supervise and carry out a plebiscite as we had previously declared" once "law and order has been restored," Nehru replied with a definitive no. When India had made a unilateral offer for a plebiscite after partition, he argued, Pakistan rejected it and instead chose to support chaos in the valley. It was that chaos that made the plebiscite unfeasible, he declared.

Pakistan's early policy in Kashmir obviously failed to result in any legitimacy for Pakistan's claim. Within its borders, however, the Pakistani state was incredibly successful in cementing Kashmir as an invaluable, indispensable and eternal part of the Pakistani national imagination. Primarily, this was a function of fervent propaganda campaigns carried out by newspapers such as *Dawn, Jang, Nawa-i-Waqt and Zamindar* as well as through radio broadcasts and publishing special pamphlets, books and plays. Several films produced in this era also carried an explicit message that Kashmir *belonged* to Pakistan and it was incumbent on the Pakistani state and society to take necessary measures to realise its integration within Pakistan.

Both Islamabad and New Delhi ceaselessly try to expunge from public imagination anything that questions, albeit remotely, their official narratives on Kashmir even when the two narratives sometimes are as divergent from truth as they are from each other.

The overarching theme pervading this propaganda was the two-nation theory that Muslims were different from the Hindus and, therefore, the two cannot live together. Within a few short years after independence, the Pakistani media had convinced the citizenry that pursuing Kashmir through any means was not only legitimate, it was also noble.

The argument was simple: Kashmir was a Muslim majority area and hence could not be ruled by Hindus. By promoting such a narrative, the Pakistani state ensured that the Kashmir question was enmeshed with the question of Pakistani identity and that both questions were framed in religious terms.

This narrative, however, translated into little bargaining power during negotiations with India. Unsurprisingly, when Liaquat Ali Khan exchanged letters with Indian and British leaders, he seldom made a reference to Islam or jihad. His arguments, instead, rested entirely on the Kashmiris' right to self-determine their political future. Pakistan posited that India had forcibly and undemocratically annexed Kashmir without taking the will of the people into account.

In the age of decolonisation, self-determination was considered a universal right and carried far more weight than the two-nation theory. Highlighting its absence as the core reason for the problem in Kashmir, indeed, forced India on the defensive. On several occasions, Nehru had to give assurances that a plebiscite would eventually take place and that the mandate of the Kashmiri people will be respected.

This apologetic Indian reaction convinced the Pakistani ruling elite that if it needed to force India to a negotiating table, it needed help—from powerful friends.

According to new York times of 1952: Sir Gladwyn Jebb, the British representative to the UN, handed a draft resolution on Kashmir to his Indian counterpart

Vijaya Lakshmi Pandit who hurriedly wrote to Nehru, telling him that Britain and the United States were prepared to take the matter to the UNGA if India did not move within the next 30 days. A debate in the General Assembly and a possible resolution against India could be a national embarrassment, she said.

Nehru was aghast. "Have the English learnt nothing at all during the last few years? I am not thinking so much of their draft resolution, although that is bad enough, but rather of the way they think they can bully us. If there is one thing that all the powers in the world cannot do, it is to bully us," he wrote in his feverish reply to Pandit.

Nehru's frustration with Britain and the US had been growing for the past couple of years. He believed British and American patronage was the chief reason why Pakistan was being abrasive towards India. The Pakistani establishment, indeed, was seeking political and military support from the two countries in return for strategic loyalty. Quickly though, the Pakistani elite realised that its efforts would have to be directed mostly towards the US as Britain had little economic and political clout left in the post-World War II era. While the sun was setting on the British Empire, the American pursuit of hegemony in the postcolonial world had just begun.

This period was also the beginning of the Cold War, the ideological conflict between the US and the Soviet Union that would last for the rest of the 20th century and engulf the entire world. Policymakers in the White House and the State Department were deeply anxious to enlarge the American sphere of influence to ensure that newly formed states did not gravitate towards the Soviet camp.

The American reaction to the first phase of the Kashmir crisis was to impose an arms embargo on both Pakistan and India. But this policy had to change with the beginning of the 1950's. As the realities of the Cold War took centre stage, American policymakers aggressively pursued the policy of "containment" against the "communist virus" and they found in Pakistan a willing partner in their pursuit of this policy in the subcontinent. In 1950, Liaquat Ali Khan publicly admitted that Pakistan would "seize the opportunity eagerly" should the US decide to give it as much importance as it gave to Turkey. Keen on developing a stronghold in the Middle East, the Americans were planning a multilateral security arrangement among Iran, Iraq and Turkey, their allies in the region. Given its geographical proximity to the Middle East, Pakistan could be included in this collective.

While Britain had reservations about including Pakistan in a Middle East collective and warned the Americans about the possible negative effects it might have on the relations between Washington and New Delhi, policymakers in the US remained determined to make Pakistan a client state. For its part, Pakistan received strong warnings from Moscow and Beijing against such an arrangement but the Pakistani establishment was adamant on securing military aid from the US.

When American Secretary of State John Foster Dulles visited Pakistan in the summer of 1953, he was deeply heartened to see Pakistan's enthusiasm to ally with his country. In December that year, American Vice President Richard Nixon visited the subcontinent and concluded that America needed to sacrifice a potential relationship with India for one with Pakistan. In 1954, Pakistan became part of the South East Asian Treaty Organization (Seato) that also included Australia, France, New Zealand, the Philippines, Thailand, the UK and the US; in early 1955, it joined the Baghdad Pact along with Iran, Iraq, Turkey, Britain and the US.

While the rebel in him might have been defiant, the politician in Nehru understood that these alliances had changed the power dynamics in South Asia. Equally importantly, the situation in Kashmir was changing and support for Pakistan was emerging among the Kashmiris. In 1953, Nehru acknowledged that a pro-Pakistan lobby was present in Kashmir valley alongside a pro-India one.

A number of political actors, including Sheikh Abdullah – who, by then, had become the prime minister of Jammu and Kashmir – also started imagining a possibly independent Kashmir. He went to the extent of stating that his government was not bound by the accession treaty signed by the Maharaja. Many in India's ruling Congress party, who considered him a friend, were shocked by the statement. New Delhi could simply not afford a popular challenge to the accession treaty. Sheikh Abdullah was, therefore, sentenced to 11 years in prison under what became the infamous "Kashmir conspiracy case."

All these developments forced Indian leaders to seek a lasting, internationally-recognised agreement over Kashmir. In May 1955, Nehru met with Pakistan's

Prime Minister Mohammad Ali Bogra and his interior minister Iskander Mirza in Delhi. Senior Indian minister Maulana Abul Kalam Azad was also present during the talks which lasted for three consecutive days.

Despite tumultuous relations between the two states, the air in the negotiation room was gracious, even hopeful. Nehru frankly admitted that the American military aid had changed security circumstances in the subcontinent since "it brought the prospect of world war to our door." Bogra, however, assured his Indian counterpart that Pakistan desired nothing but friendliness with its neighbour to the east. At one point, he even said: "India [is] a big country, the big sister of Pakistan... India should, therefore, be generous and magnanimous."

While the two states were putting up a rare show of mutual understanding, the voice of the Kashmiris was conspicuously missing from their discussions. The real question being discussed was a partition of Kashmir. Before the Delhi meeting, Pakistan's Governor General Malik Ghulam Muhammad had informally proposed that a large tract of land north of the Chenab River should be transferred to Pakistan and that Kashmir, as a whole, should come under some sort of a joint supervision by the two states.

For Nehru, these proposals were "completely impractical." The Indian side could never give up territory because the Indian constitution stipulated that the government in Delhi could not alter the boundaries of the state of Jammu and Kashmir without the consent of the state's own legislature.

While Bogra agreed that the Governor General's proposals were unfeasible, he emphasised that he could not return to Pakistan empty-handed. "Something had to be done to make [the people of Pakistan] feel that they had gained something," is what Bogra told Nehru who said India could transfer only the Poonch district to Pakistan. Bogra and Mirza sombrely announced that "if they accepted the Indian proposal, they would be blown sky-high in Pakistan."

Their concerns were not exaggerated. Many political and religious leaders in Pakistan were mobilising people for an Islamic war in Kashmir. On August 14, 1953, Chaudhry Khaliquzzaman, then governor of East Pakistan, exhorted the Pakistanis to "keep their swords shining and horses ready." Feroz Khan Noon, the then chief minister of Punjab, said in a public meeting in Lahore, two days later, that the Indian government had gone "back on [the] international understanding between the two countries" by sending troops into "a predominantly Muslim country—Kashmir."

Such provocations, mirrored relentlessly by the Pakistani press and radio, could only lead to an atmosphere full of deep acrimony where conflict was celebrated and peace was mocked as a manifestation of weakness. In 1954, a pamphlet entitled *Fatwa* was published in Pakistan which contained virulently anti-India contents with reference to Kashmir. The Indian High Commission in Pakistan requested the Pakistani government to withdraw the pamphlet. The request was turned down.

In these politically charged circumstances, Bogra and Mirza could not make any concessions without risking the fall of their government. The same militaristic narrative that the Pakistani state was actively promoting, thus, circumscribed its negotiating power.

When the two sides returned to the negotiating table the next day, Bogra produced a map of Jammu and Kashmir. It was divided into two parts: the Hindu areas which amounted to a few districts around Jammu were coloured yellow while the rest of the map was coloured green to indicate the Muslim majority areas. The Pakistani delegates suggested a "large area of the Jammu province including Poonch, Riyasi, Udhampur" could go to India along with the "possible transfer of Skardu to India."

Azad, at that point, stated that India could at best agree to concede some parts of Mirpur district alongside Poonch to Pakistan. For Nehru, the acceptance of Pakistani proposals was as good as an Indian "defeat and the dictation of terms" by Pakistan which, he said, no Indian government could accept. Mirza responded by stating that all he could do was report back to his government in Karachi. And on that inconclusive note, the negotiations ended.

Although the talks achieved nothing, they clearly depicted that Kashmir had turned into a territorial dispute. The ultimate object on the negotiating table was a map—a cartographic representation of space bereft of people and their history, identities, voices and relationships. The Kashmiri 'self' – which Pakistan ostensibly wanted to guard under the banner of Islam and which India wanted to protect under its constitution – was actually considered wholly fluid and expendable, something that could be cut up by the two states wantonly. The important question was not whether to cut Kashmir or not—it was how to go about cutting it. And so it has remained since then.

A young Zulfikar Ali Bhutto was hunched over a sprawling map of Kashmir, surrounded by the delegates he was leading as Pakistan's foreign minister. They were in the middle of the third round of talks with their counterparts from India. The first two rounds had taken place in Rawalpindi and Delhi. The agenda was now a familiar one—the drawing of a boundary that could divide Kashmir between India and Pakistan.

The Pakistani delegation was anxious. "We must draw lines on the map," they insisted. As ever, it seemed an impossible exercise. Swaran Singh, India's foreign minister and the head of the Indian delegation, drew a line on the map indicating his side's "readiness to concede in favor of Pakistan the rich forest areas in the north, on both sides of the Kishenganga River." He also suggested that India was ready to concede some more areas in the west and north of the Kashmir valley.

The Pakistani negotiators appeared shocked at the meagreness of his offer. Bhutto prepared a counter offer—only Kathua, a district on the border with Punjab, and some adjoining areas from other districts would go to India while Pakistan would be entitled to all the others areas up to Ladakh in the north-east and including Srinagar, Jammu, Udhampur and Riyasi districts. The Indians immediately shot down these suggestions as "ridiculous."

The invasion by the "Azad Forces" led to massive retaliation by the Indian military not only against

Pakistan but also within the state of Jammu and Kashmir. An intense military campaign was started to rid Kashmir of outside elements as well as any local pro-Pakistani activists.

Bhutto perhaps believed that placing such a huge demand would compel the Indians to revise their original offer, convincing them to give up more territory. Singh, however, was determined not to cede anything more than he had offered. He said he was willing to accept an end to the talks, seeing little point in another round scheduled in Calcutta that March.

The angst, the arguments and the outcome—nothing that happened in Karachi was unexpected but the world in which these talks took place was being critically transformed.

In 1958, Field Marshal Ayub Khan launched a coup d'état against the civilian government and set himself in power as the Chief Martial Law Administrator of Pakistan. His martial law regime was bent upon consolidating the central authority in Pakistan, reigning in recalcitrant provinces and establishing its writ at all costs. And, despite all the trouble at home, Kashmir figured prominently in the military government's imagination. Critical to this pursuit was the acquisition of military aid and international support against India. The US remained a crucial supporter in this regard and the Pakistani state continued to identify itself as a strategic ally of the West against the "menace of communism." Relations between India and Pakistan also soured further under the martial law regime despite some high-level talks, including a one-on-one meeting between Nehru and Ayub Khan. By 1961, public confrontations between the two states peaked with accusations flying between them.

That year also marked the inauguration of John F. Kennedy as the 35th president of the United States. His administration was keen on a rapprochement with India. Pakistan, obviously uncomfortable with such a policy, realised it could not rely merely on the United States and needed to expand its international support base. The Soviet Union was across a vast ideological gulf from Pakistan and, more importantly, had very friendly relations with India. Pakistan, therefore, began courting the People's Republic of China. Beginning with Nikita Khrushchev's denunciation of Stalin's legacy, China-Soviet relations had been rapidly worsening. By 1961, there was an official parting of ways. During this time, relations between China and India also experienced a sharp decline owing to a series of conflicts on the Himalayan border between the two countries. These conflicts eventually resulted in the 1962 Sino-Indian War.

China's anti-India stance as well as its victory in the 1962 war made China a possibly important ally for Pakistan. Internal correspondences among Indian officials in the early 1960's show their anxiety over a possible Pakistan-China secret deal and a possible Chinese involvement in Kashmir. Rajeshwar Dayal, India's high commissioner in Pakistan, went to the extent of warning Ayub Khan against befriending China. "I warned the President [of Pakistan] that if China was no friend of ours, it was much less a friend of Pakistan's. Bringing China into the Kashmir dispute would make the problem completely insoluble, for the

Chinese would be playing only their own game." He then reminded Ayub Khan of "his own views regarding China's aggressiveness and expansionism" and his declaration in November, 1959, "that Pakistan would not take advantage of India's difficulties with China."

Indian fears were confirmed when, during the very first round of Pakistan-India talks in early 1963, the Pakistani side announced having reached an agreement with China on Kashmir's border with the Chinese region of Sinkiang (now spelled Xinjiang). The Indian delegation was shocked not only at the nature of the announcement but also over its odd timing. Tensions rose between India and Pakistan exponentially when the China Pakistan Boundary Agreement was officially signed on March 2, 1963. The agreement sought to "delimit and demarcate" the boundary between China's Xinjiang region, and its proximate regions, which formed part of Kashmir under Pakistan's control and resulted in the demarcation of a new international border and a territory exchange between Pakistan and China. As a result of these developments, China ended up controlling all of the present-day Xinjiang region.

Through the agreement with China, Pakistan made two noteworthy gains. Firstly, it consolidated its relationship with China, signalling to both India and the United States that Pakistan had a powerful friend in the region. Secondly, by negotiating – and reaching an agreement – with China on a border in Kashmir, Pakistan was able to establish its sovereignty over those parts of Kashmir which it controlled. This was a major setback to Indian claims that the entirety of Kashmir was an indivisible whole and an unquestionable part of

India. Once China established its writ over the areas it had received through the agreement with Pakistan, it became virtually impossible for India to reclaim them without going to war with China.

Political leadership in India, therefore, was appalled by the Pak-China agreement and saw it as a proof of Pakistani insincerity. Almost immediately the matter was taken up in Lok Sabha, India's lower house of parliament. Nehru told the parliamentarians that Pakistan's official claims of having given up just over 2,000 square miles of territory to China were not correct. China, indeed, had gained control over 13,000 square miles—almost all those parts of Xinjiang region which during the British Raj in India had been included in Kashmir. This, he said, became possible because Pakistan had surrendered "that part of the Indian territory in Jammu and Kashmir which is under Pakistan's illegal occupation."

Countering the speeches being made in the Indian parliament, Bhutto addressed Pakistan's National Assembly and argued that the Indian attitude "confirms our genuine apprehensions that there has been no real desire on the part of India to reach an honourable and equitable settlement with us on Kashmir." As the stalemate continued, the political situation within Pakistan was rapidly deteriorating. Indian intelligence concluded, and rightly so, that Ayub Khan's regime found itself in hot waters. In a secret letter written to Commonwealth Secretary Y.D. Gundevia, India's high commissioner in Pakistan, G. Parthasarathy, quoted a highly credible Pakistani source – mentioned in the letter as Colonel Mohtarram – as saying that Ayub Khan was increasingly becoming unpopular among the masses as well as in the army. His unpopularity in the army could have been because of his corrupt dealings, his involvement in partisan politics and his ill treatment of senior officers. The Pakistani source believed an underground campaign against Ayub Khan was being run from England and was gaining strength. Given his desperate position within Pakistan, the source apprehended, Ayub Khan "might start the so-called 'Jihad' against India in the hope of consolidating his own position." The Indians, the colonel suggested, "should therefore be prepared to meet such a situation." He also warned that Pak-China relations were likely to deepen.

These reports caused grave apprehensions in New Delhi. An unstable regime in Pakistan could create trouble in Kashmir, especially if there had been some secret arrangement between Pakistan and China. On July 24, 1963, Bhutto gave a long and fiery speech in the National Assembly and claimed that "an attack by India on Pakistan would involve the territorial integrity and security of the largest State in Asia." This strengthened suspicions in New Delhi that a secret pact actually existed between China and Pakistan.

Also read: Neelum Valley: The sapphire trail

The Indians took the matter to the Americans, raising alarm over how a Pak-China alliance could wreak havoc in Kashmir. The Americans, however, assured the Indians that they had been guaranteed by the Pakistanis that there was no secret deal between Pakistan and China.

The American assurances did little to assuage Indian concerns. Over the course of the next year, relations between India and Pakistan plummeted even further. In early 1964, India redesignated the heads of state and government in Jammu and Kashmir as "governor" and "chief minister" – instead of Sadr-e-Riasat and Prime Minister – and called for the hoisting of the Indian flag on government buildings in the state instead of the state's own flag. In September that year, Pakistan followed suit in its part of Kashmir by replacing the Azad Kashmir flag at the President's House in Muzzafarabad with the Pakistani flag. Tensions burst forth in the summer of 1965 when guerrilla fighters – hailed as "mujahideen" in the Pakistani press – invaded Indian-controlled parts of Kashmir. According to Indian sources, "5,000 armed men, trained and supported by the Pakistani army had been sent in across the cease-fire line to commit arson and sabotage, to strike at our security forces and to incite the local people to rise against the Government." Pakistan vehemently denied having designed the infiltration, arguing that the "Azad Forces" which had invaded the Indian-controlled part of Kashmir was an organic and indigenous response to the Indian occupation. Pakistan also maintained that Pakistani military action in support of the "Azad Forces" was only an act of self-defence undertaken after India had violated the ceasefire line.

The UN, however, saw Pakistan as the aggressor and directed it to observe the ceasefire line and abide by the status quo. In a letter to the UN Secretary General, Ayub Khan refused to comply. "I fear that your present appeal will only serve to perpetrate that injustice by leaving the people of occupied Kashmir to the mercy of India. What is to become of the brave people of Kashmir who are fighting for their freedom? I cannot believe that it would be the intention of the United Nations to permit India to liquidate them and to consolidate its stranglehold over occupied Kashmir," he wrote.

The invasion by the "Azad Forces" led to massive retaliation by the Indian military not only against Pakistan but also within the state of Jammu and Kashmir. An intense military campaign was started to rid Kashmir of outside elements as well as any local pro-Pakistani activists. Regular Pakistani military units also entered the Indian-administered Kashmir, citing Indian atrocities there and as a declaration of support for the Kashmiri people. Concomitantly, India launched a full scale attack on Pakistan's western border near Lahore and Sialkot. The Pakistani authorities were not expecting this attack.

Pakistan immediately looked towards its allies, particularly the US and Britain, for help but the State Department did not find it prudent to support Pakistan. Ayub Khan invoked the assurances given by America in 1959, which made it incumbent on the US to provide support to Pakistan in the event of a war but the American government refused to entertain this plea and "did not accept Pakistani denials of infiltration across the ceasefire line." Shortly thereafter the American government imposed a military embargo on both India and Pakistan.

Pakistan vehemently protested against the embargo. In repeated discussions with the American ambassador to Pakistan as well as the British high commissioner, Bhutto pleaded for a re-evaluation of the policy. India, he argued, was still receiving aid from the Soviet Union whereas Pakistan was getting no arms since it relied solely on weapons from its Anglo-American allies. The embargo, thus, disproportionately affected Pakistan, greatly weakening its position. But all his pleas fell on deaf ears.

Anglo-American indifference was not for want of sympathy for the Pakistani case. Indeed, the September 6, 1965, attack on Lahore and Sialkot had convinced many in London and Washington that, while Pakistan might have initiated the conflict, it was Indian belligerence which had exacerbated it. There was also some recognition that Pakistan would need some guarantee regarding the resolution of the Kashmir issue for it to agree to a ceasefire. Tensions burst forth in the summer of 1965 when guerrilla fighters – hailed as "mujahideen" in the Pakistani press – invaded Indian-controlled parts of Kashmir. According to Indian sources, "5,000 armed men, trained and supported by the Pakistani army had been sent in across the cease-fire line to commit arson and sabotage, to strike at our security forces and to incite the local people to rise against the Government." Pakistan vehemently denied having designed the infiltration, arguing that the "Azad Forces" which had invaded the Indian-controlled part of Kashmir was an organic and indigenous response to the Indian occupation. Pakistan also maintained that Pakistani military action in support of the "Azad Forces" was only an act of self-defence undertaken after India had violated the ceasefire line.

The UN, however, saw Pakistan as the aggressor and directed it to observe the ceasefire line and abide by the status quo. In a letter to the UN Secretary General, Ayub Khan refused to comply. "I fear that your present appeal will only serve to perpetrate that injustice by leaving the people of occupied Kashmir to the mercy of India. What is to become of the brave people of Kashmir who are fighting for their freedom? I cannot believe that it would be the intention of the United Nations to permit India to liquidate them and to consolidate its stranglehold over occupied Kashmir," he wrote.

The invasion by the "Azad Forces" led to massive retaliation by the Indian military not only against Pakistan but also within the state of Jammu and Kashmir. An intense military campaign was started to rid Kashmir of outside elements as well as any local pro-Pakistani activists. Regular Pakistani military units also entered the Indian-administered Kashmir, citing Indian atrocities there and as a declaration of support for the Kashmiri people. Concomitantly, India launched a full scale attack on Pakistan's western border near Lahore and Sialkot. The Pakistani authorities were not expecting this attack.

Pakistan immediately looked towards its allies, particularly the US and Britain, for help but the State Department did not find it prudent to support Pakistan. Ayub Khan invoked the assurances given by America in 1959, which made it incumbent on the US to provide support to Pakistan in the event of a war but the American government refused to entertain this plea and "did not accept Pakistani denials of infiltration across the ceasefire line." Shortly thereafter the American government imposed a military embargo on both India and Pakistan.

Pakistan vehemently protested against the embargo. In repeated discussions with the American ambassador to Pakistan as well as the British high commissioner, Bhutto pleaded for a re-evaluation of the policy. India, he argued, was still receiving aid from the Soviet Union whereas Pakistan was getting no arms since it relied solely on weapons from its Anglo-American allies. The embargo, thus, disproportionately affected Pakistan, greatly weakening its position. But all his pleas fell on deaf ears.

Anglo-American indifference was not for want of sympathy for the Pakistani case. Indeed, the September 6, 1965, attack on Lahore and Sialkot had convinced many in London and Washington that, while Pakistan might have initiated the conflict, it was Indian belligerence which had exacerbated it. There was also some recognition that Pakistan would need some guarantee regarding the resolution of the Kashmir issue for it to agree to a ceasefire.

A defeated Amir Abdullah Niazi officially surrendered to his Indian counterpart General Aurora and in doing so announced the end of Pakistani sovereignty over what had been East Pakistan since 1947.

India's victory was complete. Militarily, the Indian army had enjoyed tremendous success and 93,000 Pakistani soldiers and officers were now in its custody. In the West, India had thwarted the Pakistan Army's initial advances in Chhamb and other parts of Kashmir and, instead, occupied several territories in Pakistan including Thar.

On the political front, India successfully dealt a debilitating blow to the religious basis of Pakistan as more Muslims lived in what became Bangladesh than in what remained of Pakistan. Internationally, too, New Delhi was hailed as a champion of democracy, freedom and humanitarianism that helped Bangladeshis get rid of an oppressive state.

The cataclysmic events of 1971 were obviously incredibly significant. Equally noteworthy is what did not happen. India, for instance, did not try to take over the Pakistani-controlled part of Kashmir. The reason was American pressure on the Indian government to refrain from taking the war into Kashmir. The Americans argued that any Indian action in Kashmir could precipitate a much larger war involving China, the US and the Soviet Union. D.P. Dhar, chairman of India's Policy and Planning committee and a key part of India's diplomatic endeavours before, during and after the 1971 war, admitted that the American intervention had prevented India from making territorial gains on the western front.

Washington, however, did nothing beyond making attempts to avoid a wider conflagration about Kashmir. It did not show any interests in intervening during the war on Pakistan's behalf. China, too, stayed out of the war. Bhutto, then serving as the president of the truncated Pakistan, made a frank and candid admission of his country's severely weakened position in a speech to the parliament on July 14, 1972: "Because circumstances were really impossible, India had all the cards in her hands and India is not a generous negotiator. They had Pakistani territory. They had East Pakistan separated from Pakistan. They had 93,000 prisoners of war. They had the threat of war trials and so they were sitting pretty, as the saying goes. What did we have in our hands? Riots, labour troubles and all sorts of internal dissensions… It was a nation completely demoralized, shattered."

The cataclysmic events of 1971 were obviously incredibly significant. Equally noteworthy is what did not happen. India, for instance, did not try to take over the Pakistani-controlled part of Kashmir. The reason was American pressure on the Indian government to refrain from taking the war into Kashmir.

He was speaking immediately after the signing of the Simla Agreement.

Earlier that year, Dhar met with the French foreign minister who asked him about the chance of a durable peace between India and Pakistan. Dhar was unequivocal. He said India wanted to sign a definitive peace agreement with Pakistan on all issues, including Kashmir. He made it clear to the French minister that "the package of peace related to overall settlement of all elements of tension and friction and that included Kashmir also."

Three days later, Dhar reiterated the centrality of the Kashmir issue to an enduring Pak-India peace during his meeting with Soviet President Kosygin. "… [I]n Kashmir we are faced with the question whether we leave this artificial line where trouble breaks out frequently or whether we should address ourselves to this problem also once and for all. Even if all other issues between the two countries are resolved but the Kashmir issue is allowed to fester like an open wound, there can be no hope of permanent peace in the sub-continent," Dhar said. The war had drastically changed the power dynamics in the subcontinent and Indian leaders were eager to take advantage of the changes. "Our presentation (on Kashmir)…should bear the stamp of our new prestige and authority," noted Dhar after his visits to France and the Soviet Union in February 1972. Indian diplomats insisted that the 1971 war rendered the 1949 ceasefire line in Kashmir obsolete. They knew they could make a beleaguered Pakistan agree to the new ceasefire line as a secure, inviolable international border.

Pakistan, too, was acutely aware of the asymmetry of power. When the negotiation started on June 28, 1972, Pakistan's newly appointed Foreign Minister Aziz Ahmed insisted that the peace agreement must demonstrate parity between the two sides. For any agreement to be accepted by the Pakistani public, he repeatedly argued, Pakistan must avoid giving the impression that it capitulated on the issue on Kashmir. But the Indian delegation was unflinching in its demand that the ceasefire line be turned into an international border and Pakistan cease insisting on the Kashmiris' right to self-determination. Indira Gandhi and Dhar, who were heading the Indian delegation, implied that there could be no movement on the prisoners of war and the withdrawal of Indian troops from parts of Pakistan's mainland unless Pakistan accepted the ceasefire line as the new border in Kashmir. With his "back against the wall," Bhutto had little choice but to acquiesce, though he was successful in convincing the Indians that the ceasefire line should be called something short of an internationally recognised border. The final agreement thus read: "In Jammu and Kashmir, the line of control resulting from the cease-fire of December 17, 1971 shall be respected by both sides without prejudice to the recognized position of either side. Neither side shall seek to alter it unilaterally, irrespective of mutual differences and legal interpretations. Both sides further undertake to refrain from the threat or the use of force in violation of this Line." The Simla Agreement was transformative in two respects. Firstly, it laid down bilateralism as a principle underpinning all future negotiations between Islamabad and New Delhi. India has always resisted interference and mediation by other states as well as by the UN when it comes to discussing and settling disputes with Pakistan. On the other hand, Pakistan would often ask the international community to intervene. With the Simla Agreement, Pakistani efforts to involve the rest of the world in dispute resolution in the subcontinent would have only weak moral and legal authority, if any at all. At least this is how India has been interpreting the agreement since 1972. Secondly, the agreement prevented both India and Pakistan from interfering in the territories owned or controlled by the other side.

Even though the Simla Agreement was put into effect, Dhar was not excited about its ability to maintain peace in the long run. What made him particularly pessimistic was the ever-present possibility of a military coup in Pakistan. Indeed, just five years after the agreement, Pakistan experienced its third coup, inaugurating the reign of the most protracted and arguably the most repressive martial law regime in the country—under General Ziaul Haq.

Over the next decade, Pakistan became a crucial player in the America-led proxy war in Afghanistan. The Pakistan Army fostered, facilitated and trained Afghan mujahideen not just militarily but also ideologically. A generation of military officers and soldiers, working with these mujahideen, came of age espousing ideas for a global jihad in general and the one in Kashmir in particular. It was during this era that the Zia regime encouraged the massive growth of Islamic fundamentalist organisations within Pakistan and actively supported the emergence of militant outfits for guerrilla warfare in Afghanistan and Kashmir.

In 1989, the Red Army began its historic retreat from Afghanistan, initiating the end of the Soviet Union and the Cold War. Emboldened by this victory, the Pakistani establishment cast its eyes on Kashmir, yet again.

The sound of gunfire and explosives reverberated in the valley mingled with vociferous chants of *'azadi.'* Young men, their faces often covered, carried Kalashnikov rifles and roamed the streets of Indian-administered Kashmir, demanding freedom from New Delhi.

The roots of the 1989 insurgency in Kashmir lay in a highly problematic history of electoral politics of Jammu and Kashmir. In 1987, Farooq Abdullah, son of Sheikh Abdullah and the leader of the National Conference, struck a deal with the Indian government led by Prime Minister Rajiv Gandhi for the resumption of the electoral process in Indian-administered Kashmir. The election that followed resulted in an easy victory for Farooq Abdullah. The only problem was that a large part of the Kashmiri population deemed the voting to be rigged. By 1989, a huge number of Kashmiri youth had risen in anger to protest against what they considered an unrepresentative government. Many of them soon joined an insurgency against the Indian state.

India was quick to respond, deposing Farooq Abdullah, installing Jagmohan Malhotra as governor and deploying 700,000 military and paramilitary soldiers in Kashmir to counter the insurgency. The insurgents received immense support – militarily, diplomatically and financially – from Pakistan. The Pakistani military, particularly the Inter-Services Intelligence (ISI), was eager to take advantage of anti-Indian sentiments within Kashmir. Jihadi outfits, including the Lashkar-e-Taiba (LT), Hizbul Mujahideen and Harkat-ul-Ansar, were propped up to recruit young Kashmiri men, bring them into Pakistan for training and then send them back into Indian-administered Kashmir.

A generation of military officers and soldiers, working with these mujahideen, came of age espousing ideas for a global jihad in general and the one in Kashmir in particular.

These developments were taking place as democracy returned to Pakistan in 1988 after an 11-year hiatus and Benazir Bhutto became prime minister. But even though she headed a civilian government, the military establishment tenaciously held on to its influence, particularly on subjects such as Kashmir. Managing relations with India, thus, became a reflection of the conflicting tendencies in Pakistani politics. While the civilian government claimed to work towards a diplomatic solution to the Kashmir issue, the military ardently supported jihadist outfits. This was not lost on the Indian government which rightly considered Benazir Bhutto's government vulnerable to pressure from the military.

It was only in January 1994 that the two sides finally agreed to resume their formal dialogue process as Pakistan's foreign secretary presented a series of non-papers – so called because the positions stated therein are not considered official – to his Indian counterpart. These non-papers proposed "measures required to create a propitious climate for peaceful resolution of the Jammu and Kashmir dispute and other issues." These measures ranged from finding the modalities for the holding of a plebiscite in Jammu and Kashmir to the resolution of other territorial conflicts such as Siachen and Sir Creek.

The Indian reply was dismissive: "India categorically states once again that Jammu and Kashmir is an integral part of India. The question or the need for conducting any plebiscite in any part of India including in the State of Jammu and Kashmir simply does not arise." The Indian side also claimed that Pakistan had only restated its preconditions for talks through the non-papers. The stalemate thus persisted.

In 1996, Farooq Abdullah once again formed a government in Indian-administered Kashmir with support from Congress. Meanwhile in Pakistan, Benazir Bhutto's second government was toppled and Nawaz Sharif became prime minister, for the second time, in 1997. Amid all these changes, relations between India and Pakistan were following what by then had become a familiar pattern: talk of peace ran parallel to talk of war.

This pattern continued when Sharif met his Indian counterpart Atal Bihari Vajpayee in September 1998 in New York on the sidelines of the UNGA. The two sides reaffirmed their commitment to bilateral dialogue during the meeting. But when, a few days later, Sharif supported Kashmir's right to independence during his address at the UN, his remarks elicited strong objections from New Delhi. His address marked two critical changes. For the first time, Pakistan supported a "third option"—of letting Kashmir become an independent state if it did not want to remain a part of India but also did not want to join Pakistan. As late as 1995, Benazir Bhutto had rejected the third option, arguing that "it would mean the balkanization of both India and Pakistan, which was not in their interest."

Secondly, both India and Pakistan became nuclear states by 1998 and their nuclear capabilities meant that the next war could lead to an unprecedented degree of destruction. The age-old question of Kashmir thus operated in a drastically new paradigm – to put it in the words of some American pundits and officials, the dispute over Kashmir became the world's most dangerous nuclear flashpoint.

It was only after many years that India was willing to come back to the negotiating table. In a historic moment, Prime Minister Vajpayee travelled by bus to Lahore. The world applauded what appeared to be a significant breakthrough. But in the ultimate manifestation of Pakistan's paradoxical and often parallel policies, the Pakistan Army started sending troops into Kargil on the Indian-controlled side of Kashmir, leading to the fourth India-Pakistan war.

The Kargil War was envisioned as a covert operation; which is why Pakistan initially stressed that an Indian assault was aimed at the Kashmiri mujahideen and that Pakistan had sent its troops to the border only in self-defence. But the massive retaliation by India – known as Operation Vijay – compelled Pakistan to seek American mediation for an immediate ceasefire. This showed India that it could neutralise a military attack by Pakistan, the latter's nuclear capability notwithstanding.

Some discussion in Washington: The American Secretary of State Colin Powell did not seem happy. In a meeting with Khurshid Kasuri, Pakistan's foreign minister, he expressed concern over the continued infiltration across the Line of Control (LoC) in Kashmir. Summer was around the corner which would make movement across the LoC easier, pushing Pakistan and India towards the brink of another violent conflict. "We would have a real mess on our hands," Powell told Kasuri. India and Pakistan, he insisted, would have to take "difficult decisions" were they to avoid war.

The American concerns were well founded. Pakistan and India had been on the precipice of a war in 2001/2002 following a terrorist attack on the Indian parliament. While the US had strengthened its relationship with India tremendously over the 1990's, a post-9/11 Pakistan was once again required as a key strategic ally in the War on Terror. America's strategic interests in South Asia and the Middle East dictated that Washington did whatever it could to keep both India and Pakistan on its side and stop them from engaging in a war. Condoleezza Rice, Powell's successor as the Secretary of State, informed Kasuri that "American regional interests were linked to stability in South Asia."

In his recently published memoir, *Neither a Hawk Nor a Dove,* Kasuri credits the Bush administration with facilitating the peace process between India and Pakistan. Pressure from the US, Kasuri reveals, compelled President Pervez Musharraf to reign in a hawkish policy towards India and create conditions conducive for something extraordinary—a chance to settle the Kashmir dispute for all times to come.

Beginning in June 2004, India and Pakistan resumed their Composite Dialogue—a process of negotiations that requires simultaneous progress on eight contentious subjects including Kashmir, terrorism, water sharing, nuclear weapons and territorial disputes. In September that year, the two sides decided to set up a mechanism for holding backchannel negotiations on Kashmir. Over the next couple of years, serving and former diplomats and officials from the two countries would hold secret meetings to come up with a formula for a negotiated settlement of the conflict. Publically, too, the two governments sought to mend relations and appeared happy with the progress they were making.

Manmohan Singh, who became India's prime minister in 2004, however, made it clear to Pakistan that the border in Kashmir could not be redrawn. It could be allowed to become "irrelevant," though, by letting the Kashmiris travel across it with ease. This eventually led to the historic opening of the Muzaffarabad-Srinagar Bus Service in April 2005.

Meanwhile, local and foreign interlocutors agreed that Pakistan's overtures for peace could only amount to something if its establishment agreed to unravel the infrastructure it had so meticulously constructed over the past decade and a half for an insurgency in Kashmir. Murmurs in 2005 and 2006 within Islamabad's most powerful circles suggested that Musharraf was indeed considering that. While active infiltration into Kashmir decreased during and after those years, terrorist incidents elsewhere in India, such as the serial train bombings in Mumbai in July 2006, still haunted the bilateral negotiations. The terrorist attack which claimed over 200 lives led to severe criticism of Pakistan, and public support in India for the dialogue process plummeted rapidly. Pakistan's official denial of any involvement in the attack as well as Musharraf's insistence that Pakistan was no longer supporting terrorist outfits creating trouble in India did little to improve the situation. This is how an official Indian spokesman summed up the situation: "If Pakistan really wants to convince the people of India that we are working against terrorism then it can take some action immediately. For example, the self-styled chief of Hizbul Mujahideen, Syed Salahuddin…should be arrested and handed over to India." The spokesman also called for an action against Jamaatud Dawa. "Instead of their saying that Jamaat-ud-Dawa is being kept under close watch, the organization should be banned and its leader should be arrested." A few months later, Musharraf met Singh in Havana and the two sides agreed to set up a joint antiterror mechanism.

In December 2006, Musharraf announced something unprecedented. Pakistan, he said, was willing to give up its claim on Kashmir should India agree to his four-point proposal which suggested that: (a) borders between Pakistan and India remain the same; (b) Kashmir be given autonomy but not independence; (c) a steady withdrawal of troops take place from both Indian and Pakistani administered parts of Kashmir and (d) a joint supervision mechanism be set up with representatives from India, Pakistan and Kashmir to ensure a smooth implementation of these proposals. Pakistan said it was even ready to take back its demand for a plebiscite if India was willing to negotiate on the proposals.

It remains a matter of conjecture if Musharraf was truly committed to a peace deal but the undemocratic nature of his regime allowed him to exhibit flexibility that a civilian government could not afford. At one stage, a bilateral agreement appeared extremely possible. "We were down to the commas," Kasuri later told Steve Coll of the *New York Times*. While Pakistan insisted it had to take into account Kashmiris' sentiment, the conspicuous absence of any Kashmiri representation in the process was hard to miss. After 60 years of going through political suppression, geographical and social divisions and wars, the Kashmiris were still largely absent from a negotiation table laid down to decide their destiny.

It would appear that Pakistan and India were on the precipice of a "deal on Kashmir" when the peace process was thwarted by the political turmoil that engulfed Pakistan in 2007 and continued well into 2008.

On November 26, 2008, 10 young men launched a massive terrorist attack in Mumbai, leading to the killing of 164 people over a period of three days. India later claimed the attackers were members of the Pakistan-based LT. The attack would extinguish the prospects of an India-Pakistan peace for many years to come.

While driving on The Mall, one is likely to spot autorickshaws carrying a certain poster on their backs proclaiming that Pakistan has the right to get Kashmir back from India. The poster also exhorts: "Pakistan can only survive if it keeps its ideology intact." Together, the two slogans have long served as the bedrock of a state-driven national narrative that sees Islam and Kashmir as its twin foundational pillars.

The pursuit of Kashmir remains embedded in popular and official imagination as strongly as the perception that a nuclear Pakistan has a special status within the Muslim countries. Both these views were manifest – and with a lot of celebratory chest thumping – as Pakistan commemorated the 50th anniversary of the 1965 War with India – a war that Pakistan still claims it won. General Raheel Sharif, Chief of the Army Staff and arguably the most powerful man in the country, partook in the celebrations, announcing that "Kashmir remains the unfinished business of partition."

Across the LoC, India's grip on Kashmir has never been stronger. With half a million soldiers stationed there, Kashmir is the most densely militarised area in the world. And enjoying an across-the-board political support for counterinsurgency measures, Indian governments of different ideological persuasions have felt no qualms in perpetuating a reign of terror against the Kashmiri civilians found protesting on the streets.

Chauvinistic and jingoistic rhetoric and policies prevail in both India and Pakistan as far as their stances on Kashmir are concerned. The two governments keep assuring their electorate of the legitimacy of their position as well as their preparedness for war.

The rest of the world, meanwhile, remains a faithful, but passive, audience to a Kashmiri spectacle, in which the same characters are condemned to perform the same acts with the same tragic outcomes.

This are history, which is been the reality of Kashmir. How the misuse of Kashmir is been happened from starting by the various leaders mentioned above. In my 2nd chapter I will take you towards the kashmiri pandit. It was also the issue been very sensational in Kashmir.

Kashmiri Pandit

In Kashmir there are many communities who live among them there is one community who is been present there in big number but they have been in very limited ratio now as compare to past. The community is Kashmiri pandit (also known as kashmiri brahamins). Past 5000 year history is been there of kashmiri pandit it is been situated from Ashoka period.

If we talk about the time after independent the records shows that the population of pandit were 6 percent in valley in the year 1947 but after 1950 its reduced to 5 percent. I am indicating this ratio because I want to indicate the fact that how fast tthat we all from he ratio of the pandit who is the citizen of the same place were getting reduce so fast. If we calculate the ratio of present time they are no more existing there. Its so sad that in our own country this kind of situation occurred. Thats only the reason I called India is free but Kashmir is still not free. Is a shame for country members that we cant make our Kashmir free till date.

They were been called as kafirs in our own Kashmir. That was too shame for each Indian that Indian our only known as kafirs in kashmir at the time of war been take place in Kashmir. No Indians were in support of them at that time.

The records say that Militants back from Pakistan plans the strategy to kill the kashmiri pandit with the slogan that they are kafirs. This was so sad that Pakistani was distracting Indians muslim mind. After reading this the question arise that why they were been distracting by the Pakistani militants. So the ans for same is they were forced by the militants to do that because they were started ruling in our own Kashmir which was been very shameful incident for each Indian. Actually at that time which Pakistani militants came back from Pakistan were started ruling in our own Kashmir.

Militants entered with help of some corrupt politicians of Kashmir which were earning bread from india but they were still serving to Pakistan. They were totally Pakistani who never wanting Kashmir in india so they stay back in Kashmir and try to create various issue in Kashmir with help of militants. The problem at the time of 1990 occur in Kashmir that each muslim were started control by Pakistani and they were been giving threats too and various fake knowledge were giving to the youth of the Kashmir that Kashmir belongs to Pakistan and its not a part of india. At the age of young you are not that much mature especially the illiterate ones which comes under control of militants. Various religion ambassador were been called by militants from Pakistan so with help of brain wash can be made by them to the youth muslim. This all are the strategy which is been create by Pakistani in Pakistan with help of politician sitting in our own Kashmir.

When they have fulfilled with the target of the biggest number in there control they started with the mission of taking out the hindu from Kashmir. They begind as I mentioned above with slogan that all hindus are kafir. So they were been helping in brain wash of the Muslim citizen of Kashmir. Through which they get unity power. With the help of the unity they were started the working on the strategy of targeting the Kashmiri pandit. So through this strategy they started focusing towards the Kashmir to make free from kashmiri pandit. This became a motive to make muslim peoples Kashmir so they can be say freely its of Pakistan not of India.

At the time of war there is been lot of trouble which is been giving to the Kashmiri pandit there. Lot of threat were been started giving to the family of pandit at the time of war by the militants. The threat were been in form of arresting them without any charge and start giving the 3rd degree and tell them to live Kashmir. That's what I mention that the politician of Kashmir only helping them to create this problem in Kashmir. Because without there support it cant be possible that these incident can be happened. I feel that's respectively it is been the responsibility of the central government also to keep an eye at the time when this been is the stage of beginning. But its a truth which been in record that the central government were not been taken the matter seriously and they wash their hand by saying that its the matter of Kashmir there leader will mange the things. So its a bitter truth that no one is in support of kashmiri pandit at the time of war.

But there was one more group of people which were in support of them I came to know when I was been busy in finding the fact for kashmiri pandit then I came to know that some people who lives together with the kashmiri pandit they stand with them. The person who were in support they were muslim community peoples. I was shocked to hear that the muslim people were in support of pandit. But it was the truth that they were in support because its true that because of some peoples benefit this religion rights is been the creation of peoples only and they don't want to stop this because the bread were been earned with help of rights only. So as I mention that the leaders were only the culprit for the war for pandit. So the community which were helping the pandit is not been digest by the militants. So militants started same strategy towards the people were not in support they started arresting the people or tried to barain wash of left onces. If they are fail for some people so they started calling them also a kafir. Ya its shocking but it is in record that muslims who was in support of pandit they were the biggest enemy of militants and the people of Kashmir who were not in support of kashmiri pandit.

Finally militants got the full power in Kashmir with the help of leaders and the people whom they make there side with there power. So they started there target to hit out the kashmiri pandit out of Kashmir with help of burning there house ans as I mention above they were having the power of Pakistan. So no one help out even central govt. Were also been very helpless because at the starting time they were been silent. So when they awake from sleep so it was too late. This I was not telling like this its been fact been mention in various record.

It was been very sad that till date lot of Rulling party is been changed in Kashmir and in central too there is been changed but no change in the situation in Kashmir and no one take pain too take back Kashmir pandit in there own house.

Now in my next chapter I will take you towards the journey of Article 370, was the fact and figures are of same.

Detail Talk on 370

So there is one more issue in Kashmir which is been the hindrance or been the biggest wall towards the growth of Kashmir that is Article 370. If we are talking to towards this so we should know exactly what is this then after I will tell you why is this been the hindrance towards the growth of Kashmir.

So article 370 is been came to India in the year 1949. 370 is the special provision given to citizen of Kashmir by the central government. This article is been came to existence because of the Sheikh Abdullah. He was the appointed Prime Minister of Jammu and Kashmir. So he want to rule over in Kashmir as a separate country. So at that time maharaja put his word to central government of India that he want an support from the India Govt. So the govt and Maharja cames with the conculsion of the Article 370. So at that time this agreement signed between central government and king Maharaja Hari singh in the presence of Sheikh Abdullah and Jawhar lal Nehru. Maharaja Hari singh was the king of jamu and Kashmir and he don't want Kashmir to be merge in Pakistan nor in India. He wants Kashmir to be next Switzerland. So India came forward and joint hands with Maharaja Hari Singh in the form of singing the Article 370. This article is been signed between

Jawaharlal Nehru and Maharaja Hari Singh in this airticle is been there is been many provision is been mentioned in the favour of people of Kashmir. There are the clause which is been mentioned in this airticle are as follow:

1. **The Jammu and Kashmir** citizens have dual citizenship.

2. The term period of Jammu and Kashmir **legislative assembly** is of **6 years** unlike that of other states of India.

3. The order of Supreme court are not valid in Jammu and Kashmir.

4. **Only a permanent resident of Kashmir can own a land in Kashmir. No outsider can have a land in Kashmir.**

5. A Women who marries an Indian of the other state would no more have its Kashmiri citizenship. Whereas if she marries a Pakistani, her citizenship will be the same (ie., of a Kashmiri)

6. Except for defence, foreign affairs and communication, all the other laws have to be passed by the State government.

7. **All the bills passed by the parliament, should also have to pass by the State government.**

   Example: The RTI can not be filed by the Kashmiri citizens because the RTI bill is not passed by the State government.

8. The Article opposes the implementation of **national emergency *and* financial emergency *under Article 352* of the Indian constitution.** The emergency can only be imposed in case of external aggression.

9. **Shariat law** is applicable for women of Kashmir.

10. RTE is also not implemented in Kashmir.

11. **Special provision under Article 35 A** allows the State to prefer the citizens for:

   - Employment under the State government.

   - Acquisition of immovable property in state.

   - Settlement in the State.

   - Right to **scholarship** and such other forms of aid as state government may provide.

Pros of the Article 370:

1. No outsider is allowed to purchase land in Jammu and Kashmir.

2. It's difficult for outsiders to establish business in Kashmir, so the citizens of Kashmir get an advantage here as there is less competition and more opportunities for the citizens.

3. Unlike Delhi NCR, there is no population blast in Kashmir because of low settlement of people of other states in Kashmir.

4. Local brands are still running.

5. Low crime rate (but high terrorism).

Cons of the Article 370:

1. Lack of medical facilities because there are less private hospitals and the condition of government hospitals are poor terrorism.

2. No industrial sector available.

3. Corruption is more in J&K than from other states.

4. Only Muslims can become Chief ministers of J&K. So the politics is run in the name of religion there.

5. Poor education and low GDP.

These are the point which is been mentioned in agreement which is clearly indicate that in this agreement the clause been mentioned is been for the citizen of Kashmir. But in this agreement it has been clearly see that the margin of benefit is been giving to Mens of Kashmir in compare too women.

As I have discussed that this Article is been the biggest wall towards the growth of Kashmir. Its clearly shows the above mentioned point of article 370 shows that the clear image of agreement that all the clause clearly indicate the Kashmir as a separate from Central govt. Means it is been the part of India is just on paper the reality is Kashmir is been totally a separate part. All the point which is been mentioned is been totally in the favour of the big leaders which is been very sad but its true as per the condition of Kashmir also clearly indicate the status.

This article is been the biggest mistake which is been done in the favour of Kashmir. At the time of singing this Article lot of leaders that time is also been not in the favour of the agreement which is been passed. It is been in record that there are been many leaders who have been forced too sit back who are not in the favour of this agreement. Few leaders of ruling party at the time of article is been signed were not in favour but then also the biggest politician of that time stop them with there power. It is been true the great leader of that time Sardar patel sahib was not in favour of this agreement but Nehru declines everyone and put his word with more politician of congress in the parliament in the favour agreement. And pass the bill in the favour of Article. This is been claim by the peoples of that time that Nehru is been pressurised by the Queen Mountbatten to pass the bill of the Article. it is the official truth that English govt send this Queen to create the disturbance among the two leaders. She do that too. Because of her only the communist right been also take place. And its been also true that Pakistan and India divided incident been also take place with the help of Queen only.

The speech which the Nehru giving in the favour of Article is: "Gopalaswamy Ayyangar has been especially asked to help in Kashmir matters. Both for this reason and because of his intimate knowledge and experience of Kashmir, he had to be given full latitude. I really do not know where the States Ministry (Sardar Patel's ministry) comes into the picture except that it should be kept informed for the steps taken. All this was done at my instance and I do not propose to abdicate my functions in regard to matters for which I consider myself responsible." This was the speech after which Sardar sahib giving the resign.

So it is been clear my point that Iron man of India was not in the favour of this article so how the growth of Kashmir been done. Because everyone knows he takes the decision in benefit of India when these peoples not in support how come the Kashmir will grow. Its been very strange that locals of Kashmir don't feel they are Indian even they don't feel like to call them as Indian. This statements were given by the local citizen only which is been mention in records of media.

As per the article 370 outsider cant invest in Kashmir it is been the big hindrance of the growth of Kashmir. Because of this clause monetary and market both are down in that case development of the Kashmir cant be possible. As we have CAG, Lokpal, CBI to investigate corruption issues in other States of India, Kashmir due to article 370 does not come under these anti-corruption bodies. When corruption is on its toll in India it becomes a very important issue of debate that since the top most investigation bodies of India does not have its operation in Kashmir, is Kashmir totally a corruption free State and does not need such authorities. It is well known to all that Pakistan is a great threat to India due to its deep involvements in terrorism. The Article also gives Pakistan's citizens entitlement to Indian citizenship, if he marries a Kashmiri girl. This is very sensitive issue and needs to be looked upon with great care and precautions. This way we are welcoming terrorists thereby making them our son in laws. How can this be justified when terrorism is not only a national issue of concern but global as well and more importantly when Kashmir is the eye of Pakistan right from the time of Independence.

People are not only deprived of right to information but also the procedure to file the complaint. Which means a very important aspect of Democracy to have a transparent government is missing from the State. RTI has proved to be a very important tool to fight corruption, in the absence of RTI it can be assumed that politicians of J&K wants to escape from accountability thereby refusing to abrogate Article 370. Fight corruption, in the absence of RTI it can be assumed that politicians of J&K wants to escape from accountability thereby refusing to abrogate Article 370. Article 370, included in the Constitution on a temporary provision should have been gradually abrogated. This has not happened in sixty years. In fact whenever someone mentions this, vested interests raise an outcry that legitimate rights of Kashmiris are being trampled upon. Stated agenda of National Conference is return to pre 1953 status. Why should a state of Indian Union have a special status? It conveys a wrong signal not only to Kashmiris but also to the separatists, Pakistan and indeed the international community that J&K is still to become integral part of India, the sooner Article 370 is done away is better.

The above mention clause are the detail talk on article 370. This are the facts which I collect from the various places and these are the truth which is been in record. All the clause directly shows how badly is 370 is influencing everyone in Kashmir. But the bitter truth is still Kashmir is not the part of india Because of this article.

Terror Funding in Kashmir

It is been also very shameful topic in the history of Kashmir, that the terrorist are still active in valley till the present date. It is been very easy to attack or been rule in Kashmir with the help of terror attack. This activity is been easily been planned in the valley. This terorist can easily be mange the activity by sitting out of Kashmir. This activity is been done with help of some local people which give support to outsider for this activity. According to the records it is been proofed that, At least 18 properties of top Hurriyat leaders linked to Lashkar-e-Taiba chief Hafiz Saeed have been identified by investigative agencies as part of the crackdown on terror funding in the valley.

A Hafiz Saeed property has also been identified in Pakistan, details of which are not mentioned in the list of properties.

Ten properties of Zahoor Ahmad Shah Watali, who is currently lodged in Delhi's Tihar jail in a terror funding case being probed by the National Investigation Agency (NIA) have been listed out among the properties that will be seized in the crackdown.

These properties were allegedly amassed by these leaders with the funding provided by Pakistan and ISI.

Hizbul Mujahideen chief Syed Salahuddin's house in a prime location in the Pakistan's capital city is also under the scanner of the agencies.

The immovable assets of separatist leaders have been identified as part of the investigative agencies' probe in multiple terror funding cases.

According to PTI, federal probe agencies like the Enforcement Directorate (ED), NIA and the Income Tax Department will soon initiate steps to attach these assets under various criminal laws by approaching the international bodies concerned.

Watali's properties include a single-storyed house at Chhanpora in Srinagar, land at Trison City, Narbal in Srinagar, a single-storyed house at Handwara, eight kanal land at Nagrota in Jammu and an under construction nursing home in Srinagar district.

Zahoor Ahmad Shah Watali's Gurgaon property has already been attached by the ED in a separate case.

The list of properties that will be attached, include the names of top separatist leaders of the valley. Apart from one property of Hafiz Saeed, two properties of separatist leader Aftab Ahmad Shah, one property of Nayeem Ahmad Khan, one of Farooq Ahmad Dar, one of Mohammad Akbar Khanday, one of Raja Mehrajuddin Kalwal and another property of Bashir Ahmad Bhat have also been identified along with the 10 properties of Watali.

Funds were provided to the leadership of Kashmir-based terrorist groups for misguiding, motivating and recruiting local youths to militant ranks, another official told PTI.

These funds are used for maintaining Hurriyat's top leadership and a massive propaganda machinery to arouse disaffection among the people of Jammu and Kashmir against the Centre.

It is been also the fact that some action been also been taken by Ed, The Enforcement Directorate (ED) imposed a penalty of Rs. 14.40 lakh on Hurriyat Conference leader Syed Ali Shah Geelani under the Foreign Exchange Management Act. They also confiscated around Rs. 7 lakh ($10,000) that were seized from his premises during an Income Tax raid at his residence in Srinagar's Hyderpora area in 2002. The penalty was imposed under the Foreign Exchange Management Act.

ED also confiscated the money seized from his premises during an Income Tax raid in 2002.

Last year, the ED summoned Syed Ali Shah Geelani for adjudication proceedings related to the foreign exchange violation case.

Jammu and Kashmir authorities have placed senior separatist leader Mirwaiz Umer Farooq under house arrest in Srinagar.

The development comes ahead of post-Friday prayers protests called by separatists against the custodial death of Rizwan Asad Pandit, a 28-year-old private school teacher, on Monday.

On Thursday, National Conference leaders Ali Muhammad Sagar, Nasir Sogami and others took carried out a protest march from the Nawa-e-Subha party headquarters here demanding stern action against those responsible for Pandit's death.

According to the police, Pandit was arrested last week in connection with a militancy related case.

NIA had issued a summon to the Mirwaiz to appear before the agency headquarters in the national capital in a case related to funding of terror and separatists organisations in the Kashmir Valley.

However, Mirwaiz Umer Farooq did not appear before the NIA in New Delhi and said he was willing to be quizzed in Srinagar as he feared for his security in the national capital. The National Investigation Agency has secured recorded confessional statements on the flow of money, especially from Pakistan, from two persons accused in a case related to the funding of terror activities in Kashmir.

These are all the proofs which shows some action been taken towards the terror funding. But as I mentioned there is been lot of help been giving to them by the politician of Kashmir only so what the various investigation agenise can do if the proofs are been destroy with the help of leaders only. So let's take you towards the next chapter in which I will discuss "How the youth and children is been distracted by the terrorist."

Child Exploited
for Terrorism

When I was been taking a walk in Kashmir I get through with bitter situation of young kid in Kashmir. I have seen the small kids taking stones on hand ready to hit on the civilians. When get through with this in details I find lot of facts which shows the growth rate of children involving in terrorism. There is been the big issue that the terrorist are been easily successful towards the distracting the children mind towards there mission. Its been also very shameful incident for us that small kids our been involved with terrorism it can be only possible because we are fail to give the proper education. Our government are still lacking to give education in Kashmir. Kids are not travelling towards the school. When I get through in detail I find that the family of child is also been responsible in making the child been involving in terror activity. Because the parents are only the person who's been known as the first teacher and they are only being the biggest hindrance of the child education. Yes is been true that they are not supporting anyone for there child education. Some efforts been shown by govt but the parents didn't support the govt. But the real fact is been also there that the proper initiative is not been given by the govt they are not been making in the effective law towards the education so the parents are been force to make the child study and through which the growth rate of been children involving in terror activity been in lesser rate through the education. Whereas other rule been made in Kashmir in favour of political leaders. But for which the proper rule is to been make there always been lack of attention been given by the govt. Some facts which shows how important role is been children are given towards terrorism and terrorist are been getting profit with the help of children. According to the records there have been many facts and figures which proofs the growth rate of increasing child terrorist.

First question that comes up is, why these children joined terror ranks at an age when they were supposed to be going to the school and playing with the children of their age group.

Why these children joined terror ranks at an age when they were supposed to be going to the school and playing with the children of their age group. Some experts believe that the children of war cherish the desire to seek self-determination that is motivating them to join terror organisations. The glamour and idolisation of terrorists is also one of the major factors that is acting as glue for these young children to gun culture. Sheikh Showkat Hussain, a political commentator from Kashmir says that, "It's a social phenomenon that is passing from one generation to next. No one is forcing them to pick up arms."

But then another question comes up, what is the role of parents, teachers, civil society and religious leaders under such circumstances? Are they not responsible for shaping the future of the children? Why should they not own the responsibility to prevent children from the path of violence instead of blaming government for every ill within the society?

Parenting is not the responsibility of the government. It is the responsibility of the parents to ensure that the children are insulated from the toxic surroundings and made to realise what is in their best interest. It is not possible that parents or the siblings do not know what the children are upto. Under noxious surroundings the parents have to be more vigilant to ensure that the children do not become victims of radicalization or motivated by terror ideologues to pick up arms. Good teac...teaching is at the core of counter-radicalisation, teachers in the schools and colleges can identify gaps in intervention and prevention or radicalisation.

Similarly, the teachers invariably know what their pupils are up to. How often do they bunk classes and where do they spend their time. If there is a communication between parents and the teachers, the menace of children going astray to a great extent can be curbed. However, if the teachers themselves are party to the crime, in that case it is a societal problem that society needs to fix within.

Where is Kashmiri society? What role is it playing to break the cycle of violence? Similarly, what role is being played by religious teachers and seminaries? Are they not responsible to guide the youth and prevent them from taking the path of violence? Are they not supposed to make people and children aware of their responsibility as a citizen and true Muslims? Instead of asking youth to come out and indulge in stone pelting and then create conditions where security forces are compelled to ac t in self-defence, why civil society is not holding these radicals accountable for murder of youths? Why is the civil society quiet about such contempt by the religious leaders and separatists? The civil society and religious organisations have played a dubious role because no one has asked them the question what they have done to prevent Kashmir become next Syria or Afghanistan. It is most unfortunate that the failure of parenting, failure of the teachers to reform their wards, the blame is shifted to the government and security forces for their culpability. Instead of taking ownership of reforming the society, society elders and religious leaders are pointing fingers at the government and security forces. Job of reforming a society is not the responsibility of the government and the security forces. They can only assist if society and religious institutions come forward to take up the responsibility to fix societal problems.

In fact Mudasir and Saqib Bilal were not killed by security forces but these young children were failed by their parents, teachers, civil society and religious leaders who could not understand the predicament of the impressionable minds. Thus the blame cannot be shifted to the security forces and the government. The cycle of violence, and taking the children off the street is the sole responsibility of these four key institutions.

One must ask the questions from the religious leaders, teachers and elders of the society, how many terrorists they brought back or created environment for them to surrender? They cannot sit on the sidelines and pass judgment on the actions of security forces for their own failure? There is no evidence of any one of these institutions having stood up against the terror ideologues or radicals to stop radicalisation of their children. Who can pick up early signs of radicalization? There is no simple. model of easy-to-spot signs of "radicalisation."

However, if someone can spot radicalisation or change in behavior of a child, it is parents, teachers and the Mollavi. It is really not possible that all of them fail to identify early signs of radicalisation. But if teachers and religious leaders themselves act as recruiter, in that case society is doomed and the blame cannot be put on the state and security forces. It is an investment to reclaim a radicalized youth than to eliminate him. As part of standard operating procedure, it has been sincere endeavor of the security forces to get surrender of the terrorists. Without exception the local commanders regularly interact with the parents, mollavis and elders to ensure that the young children are encouraged to return back. Even mothers and sisters are repeatedly being asked to contact their sons and brothers to return back with an assurance that they would not be harmed if they shun the path of violence. However, either due to fear or stigma of parents of surrendered Jihadi more often hold the parents back. The role of security forces and the state is limited in reclaiming the radicalized youth. The government can only assist in rehabilitation and reformation of the surrendered terrorists. The government and security forces cannot replace or assume the responsibilities of parents, teachers, religious leaders and the civil society.

Thus it is high time that the government, parents body, religious leaders and civil society elders sit down together to fix this downslide and make collective efforts to keep the children off the streets and insulate them from toxic environment.

Research on education in conflict zones has shown that schools can play a vital role in combating extremist ideas. But in order to do this pupils need to engage across communal boundaries and learn how to challenge ideas. Difficult conversation need to take place and teachers need to feel confident in leading them.

So accordingly it is been clearly shows that all the efforts are been more over required to be given by the brave teachers, parents and religious leaders who can prevent children joining the terror ranks. Now lets us movie towards our new chapter a journey of an army been present in Kashmir. I will discuss in detail the problems occurs to an army in Kashmir.

Army Deployed in Kashmir

The Indian army which is been deployed in Kashmir have been facing many problems. There are many hindrance in between because of which they cant perform there duty as they want to in Kashmir. Over the last three-and-a-half decades that the army has been deployed in the Valley, this question has taken many meanings and forms, ranging from marauding, ruthless troops to being a force of stability in a difficult, violent situation. Today, when the situation in the Valley is being compared with the late 1980's and 1990's when the army moved in large numbers, what's easily forgotten is the interregnum. The Army is, today, a part of daily life in Kashmir. New generations of Kashmiris have grown up living next door to military camps while the army, too, has learnt more about dealing with the Valley. It has sought to wean off the occupation force tag through institutional responses, making the point that it has robust and fair mechanisms to deal with errant actions, regardless of rank and order. To this end, it has shown willingness to open itself up to public scrutiny and debate where needed, trying to protect its operational privileges in the Valley guaranteed by the Armed Forces (Special Powers) Act (Afspa). But behind this iron wall, the one narrative that the Indian Army has worked hard to cultivate is that of its own ethos rubbing off on local life. The army has always lived in this strong self-belief that regardless of what anyone says or does, as an institution, it has always won the hearts and minds of people insurgency – hit areas. So, when the Naga regiment does well in Kargil operations, it becomes a moment of glory for this narrative—a story of how the Nagas, identified with insurgent groups, were recruited, trained and equipped to fight for India.

Lt. Ummer Fayaz represented that part of the narrative in Kashmir for the Indian Army. Which is why his killing has hurt the army more than all the sloganeering and assertions of it being an occupation force. In other words, Fayaz symbolised all that the army believes it has got right in Kashmir. The constant internal refrain within the army is that the last three decades have seen many of the likes of Burhan Wani in the Valley capturing the imagination of a particular generation at that time but never an alternate hero. Wani also had his impact on this generation of Kashmiris. He became a poster boy of the Kashmiri struggle all over again with the Pakistan establishment highlighting his case in capitals across the world. This time, however, India, too, has a Kashmiri face in Fayaz, one that the army believes is a result of its efforts. When close to 20,000 young men turn up at its recruitment fairs, the army views it a statement of confidence. The belief among the forces appears quite strong that left to their own, Kashmir's youth will take up employment opportunities in large numbers. So, the parallel with the past may be appealing but the situation on the ground is clearly not in the same league. What does this add up to? Fayaz's killing is bound to strengthen the military's resolve even further. It will dig its heels in and want authority to deal with any violent situation. The test for the government will be on whether to provide that legal comfort within the Afspa by way of fresh legislation or amendment after the recent Supreme Court order on allowing first information reports (FIRs) to be registered on encounters. Yes, the Valley is probably set up for difficult times given the acrimony between India and Pakistan. But Fayaz's killing has changed the complexion of the pitch completely. The Indian Army believes that it's own story is on test now and it simply cannot let things slide back. Essentially, the Indian Army locates itself within the country's democratic narrative and is increasingly using those tools to register protest or to counter allegations of excess, or, for that matter, even to address veteran welfare issues. This is a gradual but impressive evolution of a colonial army into a democratic civilian controlled one, quite different from some of the other armies in the subcontinent that shares the same roots. So, when described as an occupation force in the Valley, the Indian Army has tried to respond with its own reach-out. After all, just like those who pulled out an unsuspecting Fayaz from a wedding, there was also an insider who helped the Army and gave up Wani. And, to that extent, for the army, the battle lines in the Valley are drawn between the idea of Fayaz and the narrative of Wani—a cause they believe is worth fighting for.

Most of army men in the valley are from Rastriya Rifles all for Counter insurgency ops. 36 RR battalions are in Kashmir valley and 22 RR in the Jammu region. Earlier most CI ops were carried out by army, but since then even J&K police carries out CI ops. Hence, since 1999 a lot of RR battalions were de-inducted. Rest of army troops are posted in LoC targeting Pakistan, while BSF mans the International border. There are also a number of Para commandos posted to carry out strikes behind Pakistani lines. Marine commandos from the navy are posted across the lakes such as wular lake. Since the pace of security operations are very high in J&K, most forces have their own intelligence units and IB officers only work in advisory capacity or high level coordination, R&AW has some field intelligence posts near the LoC. Crowd control is never done by Army. So this is how the army been working in Kashmir. I would like to salute to the army of Kashmir for working so hard because of them we all are been relaxed.

Lets move on to the next chapter of mine which is been the last chapter in which I will take you towards the beauty of Kashmir.

Detail Talk on Beauty of Kashmir

At last chapter of mine I will be taking all of you towards the beauty of jammu and end my journey and go back with beautiful beauty of Kashmir in my and all my readers mind.

Jammu and Kashmir, India's one of the most picturesque state lies on the peaks of Himalayan Ranges with varying topography and culture. Jammu was the stronghold of Hindu Dogra kings and abounds with popular temples and secluded forest retreats. Kashmir's capital city, Srinagar offers delightful holidays on the lakes with their shikaras and houseboats.

Kashmir, the upper most alpine region of North India's the ethereal cold desert that goes by names such as "The Last Shangrila," Moonscape, Little Tibet and so on. Ladakh is an endearing abode of scenic charisma and diverse adventure activities like rafting, jeep safari, water sports and much more. Nestling in the lap of the dazzling, snow-capped Himalayas, the Kashmir valley is undoubtedly a jewel in India's crown. An inspiration for so much art, music and poetry, Kashmir is also honeymooners' paradise, a nature lover's wonderland and a shopper's dream come true. Over the years, Kashmir tourism has come a long way, to love and look after its tourists, fulfilling their every whim. Tourists are everywhere, soaking up all that Kashmir has to offer – the walks, the pony treks, the shikara rides at sunset on the Dal lake…and once you have visited Kashmir,, you will agree that what began as a dream, lives on as an unforgettable experience. Set like a jeweled crown on the map of India, Kashmir is a multi-faceted diamond, changing its hues with the seasons – always extravagantly beautiful. Two major Himalayan ranges, the Great Himalayan Range and the Pir Panjal, surround the landscape from the north and south respectively. They are the source of great rivers, which flow down into the valleys, forested with orchards and decorated by lily-laden lakes.

The Mughals aptly called Kashmir 'Paradise on Earth' where they journeyed across the hot plains of India, to the valley's cool environs in summer. Here they laid, with great love and care, Srinagar's many formal, waterfront gardens, now collectively known as the Mughal Gardens. Anecdotes of four and five centuries ago describe their love for these gardens, and the rivalries that centered around their ownership. They also patronized the development of art & craft among the people of Kashmir, leaving behind a heritage of exquisite artisanship among these people and making the handicrafts of the land prized gifts all over the world.

Kashmir is a land where myriad holiday ideas are realised. In winter, when snow carpets the mountains, there is skiing, tobogganing, sledge-riding, etc. along the gentle slopes. In spring and summer, the honey-dewed orchards, rippling lakes and blue skies beckon every soul to sample the many delights the mountains and valleys have to offer. Golfing at 2,700 m above the sea, water-skiing in the lakes and angling for prized rainbow trout, or simply drifting down the willow fringed alleys of lakes in shikaras and living in gorgeous houseboats are some of the most favoured ones.

Kashmir has four distinct seasons, each with its own peculiar character and distinctive charm. These are spring, summer, autumn and winter.

Spring, which extends roughly from March to early May, is when a million blossoms carpet the ground. The weather during this time can be gloriously pleasant at 23 degree Centigrade or chilly and windy at 6 degree Centigrade. This is the season when Srinagar experiences rains, but the showers are brief.

Summer extends from May until the end of August. Light woollens may be required to wear out of Srinagar. In higher altitudes night temperatures drop slightly. Srinagar at this time experiences day temperatures of between 25°C and 35°C. At this time, the whole valley is a mosaic of varying shades of green – rice fields, meadows, trees, etc. and Srinagar with its lakes and waterways is a heaven after the scorching heat of the Indian plains.

The onset of autumn, perhaps Kashmir's loveliest season, is towards September, when green turns to gold and then to russet and red. The highest day temperatures in September are around 23°C and night temperatures dip to 10°C by October, and further drop by November, when heavy woolens are essential.

Through December, to the beginning of March is winter time, which presents Srinagar in yet another mood. Bare, snow-covered landscapes being watched from beside the warmth of a fire is a joy that cannot be described to anyone who has not experienced it. Some houseboats and hotels remain open in winter-these are either centrally heated or heated with 'bukharis,' a typically Kashmiri stove kept alight with embers of wood, quite effective in the winter.

Beautiful mosques and gardens. The Sikhs overthrew the last Muslim ruler in the reign of Maharaja Ranjit Singh in 1819. In 1846 the Dogras secured the sovereignty of Kashmir from the British under the Treaty of Amrjtsar, and in 1947 the state of Jammu and Kashmir with Srinagar as its capital, became part of the Indian Union.

Today Srinagar is a resort for the tourist who can experience, at first hand, the peculiar beauty of the valley that has attracted the Chinese, the Mughals and the British to it.

Its waterways with their own quaint lifestyle, the unique Houseboat, the blossoming gardens, water sports activities, shopping for lovingly hand-crafted souvenirs and the nearby resorts make it a cherished spot among those looking for a memorable holiday.

Many tourists are attracted to Srinagar by the charm of staying on a houseboat, which provides the unique experience of living on the water in a cedar-panelled elegant bedroom, with all the conveniences of a luxury hotel. Srinagar's thousand or so houseboats are moored along sections of the Dal and Nagin Lakes and river Jhelum, each decorated fancifully and named romantically and even whimsically. Like hotels, houseboats vary in degree of luxury and have been accordingly graded by the Department of Tourism. A luxury houseboat, like a luxury hotel has fine furniture, good carpets and modern bathroom fittings, while the 'D category' (the lowest category) of houseboats, like low-budget hotels, is spartanly furnished. Like hotels too, houseboats vary widely in their locations. Some overlook the main road, others look out onto lotus gardens and yet others face tiny local markets and villages, all right in the middle of the lake! All houseboats, regardless of category, have highly personalized service. Not only is there always a "houseboy" for every boat, but the owner and his family are never far away. The cost per day of hiring a houseboat includes all meals and free rides from the houseboat to the nearest jetty and back, as no houseboat on the lakes is directly accessible from the banks.

Every standard houseboat provides a balcony in the front, a lounge, dining room, pantry and 3 or more bedrooms with attached bathrooms. All houseboats not moored to the bank of the river or lakes provide a shikara as a free service from the houseboat to the nearest ghat (jetty). Virtually every houseboat in Srinagar has been provided with a municipal water connection.

Category and location of houseboats, the State Tourism Department has classified the houseboats into five categories – Deluxe, A, B, C and D, corresponding more or less to the degree of comfort and service of hotels.

There are 1087 registered houseboats in Srinagar of which 702 are anchored in the Dal Lake, 173 in the

Nagin Lake, 142 on the River Jhelum, 5 on the Dal Lake near Naseem Bagh, and the rest in other water bodies. Among these, 349 houseboats with a combined capacity of 1007 double rooms are in the Deluxe class and are mainly anchored in Dal Lake, Nageen Lake, and Naseem Bagh. In addition there are 129 A-class houseboats, 124 B-class houseboats, 134 C-class houseboats and 351 D-class houseboats.

As I discussed this journey of mine was much more memorable as I have wrote this book at the time of my visit only. So this was the Kashmir through my book I have tried to discuss all about Kashmir all small and big point I have discussed in this book. Hope you all like the journey of Kashmir. At last I want to pray for Kashmir that coming years we get the Kashmir better and the citizens of Kashmir feel more secure live in free Kashmir. So I now I am living Kashmir going back to home hope you all also travelled with me and enjoy the journey of Kashmir with knowing of some fact of Kashmir. I will again like to come to Kashmir and when Kashmir feel be free from negative people and the beauty will shine more at time I will be coming back with u all and take one more walk in Kashmir.

9 781645 872214